# GOD'S TESTIMONY AND WAY

Stephen Kaung

Available from:

Christian Testimony Ministry
4424 Huguenot Road
Richmond, Virginia 23235

www.christiantestimonyministry.com

Printed in USA

# CONTENTS

# CHAPTER 1: THE TESTIMONY OF JESUS

*Revelation 1:17-18—And when I saw him I fell at his feet as dead; and he laid his right hand upon me, saying, Fear not; I am the first and the last, and the living one: and I became dead, and behold, I am living to the ages of ages, and have the keys of death and of hades.*

May we have a word of prayer:

*Dear Lord, as we gather together in Thy name, how precious it is to be assured of Thy presence with us. We do realize, Lord, that we are standing on holy ground. Teach us how to remove our shoes, take the place of Thy bondslaves, looking to Thee to reveal Thy mind to us that we may serve Thee as we ought. Lord, we do realize this is a holy time. We pray that Thou wilt put our flesh under the cross that every one of us will be face to face with Thee in this holy environment. Speak Lord,*

*Thy servants heareth. We ask in the name of our Lord Jesus. Amen.*

## THE QUESTION

As we are gathered together unto the Lord there is a question and there is an answer. The question was asked to Adam by God: "Where art thou?" (Genesis 3:10a) I believe even today this is the question that the Lord is asking each one of us: "Where are we, brothers and sisters?" Are we where we ought to be? Are we anxious to meet the Lord for fellowship? Or are we hiding ourselves from the Lord? It is a valid question and one which we should ask ourselves every day. The Lord is coming. He wants to have fellowship with us. Do we welcome His fellowship? Are we looking for His return and ready for Him? Where are we?

## THE ANSWER

Thank God for the answer that the little boy Samuel gave to the Lord. In spite of his youth and innocence, he did have a heart for the Lord, so he answered the Lord: "Here I am; speak." Are we here with such an attitude? Can we say from the very depths of our heart, "Lord, speak, we are here"? I think if we assume this attitude, this will be a very blessed time. As we meet with the Lord these days, may we continue to maintain such a heart attitude before the Lord. Do not think that we have heard all these things before, but may we have a heart hungry and thirsty for Him, longing for Him that whatever His Word may be, we may hear and we may obey. This is a preparation for every one of us.

## GOD'S TESTIMONY AND WAY ARE OUR FOUNDATION

Our theme is God's testimony and way. I realize that over the years we have been repeating this theme in several different ways. Therefore, when we hear it, we may think that we have already heard it more than once. Why should we repeat it again and again? And this is the question I have asked myself. I think the answer is that God's testimony and way are so essential. On the one hand it is very basic; it is our foundation. If our foundation is not firmly set, how can we go through the stormy time today? Yet, on the other hand, I believe nothing is more sublime than God's testimony and way because this is related to God's eternal purpose. Even before the foundation of the world, before there was anything except God, He purposed a purpose according to His good pleasure. This is something that pleases Him deeply.

## GOD'S ETERNAL PURPOSE

What is that purpose? This is God's testimony. He wants to testify to the world what is uppermost in His heart, what He is going to do, how He will deal with us, and what will satisfy Him. This is not just something basic; it is something profound.

Even before the foundation of the world, He purposed a purpose in His heart. The Bible says that when He purposed it, it was according to His good pleasure; and it is still that which pleases Him. What is that purpose? He wants to glorify His Son. If we were able to look into the heart of God, we would see nothing there but His Son because everything is in His Son. This is God's testimony: "Behold, My Son." If this is God's will, is it our life pursuit?

## GOD TESTIFIES OF HIS SON

You will recall that when our Lord Jesus was on earth, God testified of Him again, again, and again! After our Lord Jesus was baptized at the Jordan River, He came out of the water and the heavens opened. A voice from heaven spoke: "This is My beloved Son in whom I am well pleased" (see Matthew 3:13-17). Here we find a Person. After the ministry of Malachi the heavens were closed for four hundred years; God was silent to the world. He was even silent to His own people who had driven Him to silence. But when our Lord Jesus was baptized, the heavens opened, and the voice from heaven said, "This is My beloved Son in whom I am well pleased." Why was it so? His only begotten Son, the heir of all things was willing to leave His glory and come into this world, take up the form of a man, and live for God to accomplish His purpose and bring God's salvation. He took the place of a sinner that needs repentance and baptism. God testified of His Son.

## THE MOUNT OF TRANSFIGURATION

When our Lord Jesus was on the Mount of Transfiguration, He had already lived His life for God. There on the Mount of Transfiguration His glory appeared. And Moses and Elijah appeared to talk with Him about His exit. In other words, He had come into this world, the Word became flesh, and now He was going to leave this world or take His exit from it. How was He going to take His exit? So far as He Himself was concerned, He was ready to leave. He had come into the world according to the Father's will. He had done everything according to His Father which would please Him. Now He had the glory of leaving this world and returning to His Father. He had every right to do it. So Moses and Elijah talked with Him about His exit: "How are You going to leave this world?"

Brothers and sisters, do we know this exciting moment? Do we know that moment which concerns us for eternity? So far as our Lord Himself was concerned, He was ready to exit from the Mount of Transfiguration; but if He did, what would happen? There would be only one Man in heaven even today. Thus we would have no hope and would be condemned and eternally lost. But thank God, He did not exit from the world from the Mount of Transfiguration. He was willing to come down from the mountain, go to Jerusalem, and from there to Calvary's cross. No wonder the heavens opened and a voice came from heaven: "This is My beloved Son, hear Him." Do not talk. Do not have your own ideas or opinions, however good they may be. Hear Him. He is the One who is worthy to be heard. Are we hearing Him? (see Matthew 17:1-9a)

## JESUS' LAST ENTRY INTO JERUSALEM

In John 12 we find His last entry into Jerusalem. It was a glorious entry. Even the Gentiles wanted to see Him; so it seemed as if the world was after Him. But our Lord Jesus knew people very well. He said, "When a grain of wheat falls into the ground and dies, it bears much fruit" (see v. 24). He is that grain of wheat which fell from heaven into the ground—not to live but to die—that He may bring forth much fruit. This is how we are here this morning. He

7

said, "Father, glorify Thy name. I came for this moment with the cross in view." The heavens opened and said, "I have both glorified it and I will glorify it again" (see vv. 27-29). This is the Son, this is the Lord Jesus, this is our Savior, this is our Lord, and this is God's testimony.

## JESUS TESTIFIES OF HIMSELF

In John 8 our Lord Jesus said, "I am the light of this world." The scribes and Pharisees immediately said, "You testify of Yourself; therefore, Your witness is not true." But our Lord Jesus said, "Even if I testify of Myself, My witness is true because your law says that the witness of two or three is sure. I am testifying of Myself, but My Father who is with Me, whom you cannot see because you do not know Him, is also testifying of Me."

## THE TESTIMONY OF JOHN THE BAPTIST

The Lord said, "You liked John the Baptist. He was like a light, and he testified of Me" (see John 5:33-35). When the Lord Jesus went to be baptized, somehow John the Baptist sensed in his spirit: "This is the One of whom I should be baptized instead of me baptizing Him." John refused to baptize Him, but Jesus said, "Do it for righteousness sake." John said, "When He came out of the water, I saw the Spirit of God come down upon Him like a dove and dwell in Him. This is the Son of God" (John 1:32-34). And one day when John the Baptist was standing with two of his disciples, he saw Jesus pass by and he testified, "Behold the Lamb of God!" This is the testimony that John the Baptist gave of our Lord.

## THE OLD TESTAMENT TESTIFIES OF THE LORD JESUS

After the Lord was resurrected from the dead, two disciples left Jerusalem to go to Emmaus. They were disappointed and their hearts were broken. As they were on the way they talked about what happened. Suddenly a Man appeared and walked with them and said, "Why are you so sorrowful?" They said, "Did you not hear what happened in Jerusalem?" So they told Him. The Lord said, "How slow of faith is your heart! Doesn't the Old Testament testify of My resurrection?" He began to go through the Psalms and the Prophets and the books of Law to show them how the Scriptures testified of Him. "Ye search the Scriptures. Ye think there is eternal life in it but you do not come to Me because the Scriptures testify of Me" (see Luke 24).

On that very day in Jerusalem, He appeared to His disciples and from the book of Moses through Psalms and the Prophets, He showed them how the Scriptures spoke of Him (see Luke 24:44-45).

## THE APOSTLES TESTIFY OF THE LORD JESUS

In Acts 2 on the day of Pentecost the apostles also stood up and testified that God had anointed the Lord Jesus as Lord and Christ. There is no doubt what God's testimony is. What does God testify to? Whom does He testify to? Everything from God testifies of our Lord Jesus. Hence, it is of tremendous importance to us to know what the testimony of Jesus is.

# THE TESTIMONY OF JESUS IN THE BOOK OF REVELATION

I believe there is no better testimony than when we come to what the Lord said of Himself in Revelation 1. You will recall that the apostle John was exiled to the island of Patmos because of the Word of God and the testimony of Jesus. At the end of the first century John was the only one of the twelve apostles living at this time. He had been ministering faithfully to the churches in Asia Minor when he was exiled to that island. On the Lord's day, as we visualize him, he must have been looking across the Aegean Sea to the shores of Asia Minor because on a good day he could see the seashore. He must have been thinking about these churches that he had been ministering to before he was exiled. Suddenly he heard a voice behind him. He turned around and tried to see the voice, and he saw what we call the Patmos vision.

## THE VISION OF THE RISEN LORD

John saw seven golden lampstands which represented the seven churches in Asia Minor. Among these seven lampstands he saw One like the Son of God. Now John was most familiar with our Lord Jesus while He was on earth. I think we can safely say that of all His disciples John was the one closest to the Lord and knew the Lord better than anyone else. Even when you read the Gospel according to John, you see that it is different from the other three gospels. Four of them record the life of our Lord Jesus, but the recording of John is different; it is deeper, revealing more in the inward. He knew the Lord better than anyone else, yet when he saw that Patmos vision, he was stricken as though dead. So we see how powerful that vision is because it is the vision of the risen Lord.

## THE WORK OF OUR LORD JESUS IN HEAVEN

We know the work of our Lord Jesus when He was on earth. We know how He accomplished the work of redemption for our sake. We know His sufferings for us. But do we know what He is doing in heaven?

I remember this story about an elderly sister who was illiterate. She believed in the Lord Jesus and asked for baptism. According to the custom of that time, anyone who asked for baptism had to be examined to see whether their faith was real or not. So one day, she was brought before the elders and they began to examine her faith. One of the questions they asked was this: "What do you think the Lord Jesus is doing in heaven?" That sister thought for a while and then said, "The Lord Jesus is looking down from heaven at me trying to see what sin I have committed." Of course, she did not pass.

Now brothers and sisters, do we know better? We may be well familiar with what the Lord has done on earth, but do we know what the Lord is doing in heaven? On the cross He said, "It is finished!" The work of redemption is finished—nothing can be added. It is eternal—eternally effective. When our Lord Jesus ascended to heaven, the Bible says that He sat down at the right hand of God. We know that we do not sit down until our work is done, but after our work is done, we sit down and rest. So what do you think our Lord is doing in heaven? Is He dozing because He has nothing to do? Of course not! He is as busy as He was on earth. He is making intercession for those who come to Him that He may save them to the uttermost (see Hebrews 7:25). In other words, He is applying His finished work on the earth to our lives that we may be brought into the reality of all that He has done for us.

## THE LORD JESUS IS EXAMINING THE CHURCHES

The Lord Jesus was there standing among the seven golden lampstands. However, He was not just standing there; He was actually examining every one of these churches. He said, "I know." He is the great High Priest, but not only for us individually.

Brothers and sisters, I often feel that God's people today may know a lot of what our Lord Jesus has done on earth but may not know much of what He is doing now in heaven. As a matter of fact, if we do not know what He is doing in heaven, we cannot walk the Christian walk. That is impossible. More so, we do not know what He is doing to the churches. He said, "I will build My church and the gates of Hades shall not prevail against it." Our Lord did not begin to build the church until after He died, was resurrected, and had ascended. When He was on earth, He was preparing materials for the church. However, He was not building the church because it did not begin until the day of Pentecost. After He ascended, He was anointed by the Father as the Lord, the Christ. The oil fell on His head, came down His beard onto His whole body. This is Pentecost. There were one hundred and twenty believers—the best you can know—but nevertheless it was one hundred and twenty individual believers, a congregation. But on the day of Pentecost, a tremendous change came. In one Spirit they were baptized into one body. Therefore, do not look at the sound and the sight of Pentecost. Do not be occupied with the blowing of the wind or the hard breathing of a person. Do not be occupied with the fire as tongues falling upon the heads. These are secondary events and complimentary. They may happen, but they may not. But what happened at Pentecost is of tremendous value because in one Spirit we have been baptized into one body. That is the beginning of the church.

# THE LORD JESUS IS BUILDING HIS CHURCH TODAY

Dear brothers and sisters, the building of the church began after His death, resurrection, ascension. That is what our Lord is doing today. He is building His church. He is looking at every one of these seven churches as representatives of the churches in the first century as well as the churches throughout the centuries even today. Our Lord is diligently ministering to build up His church.

The way He is building His church struck John almost to death. Brothers and sisters, I am in fear and trembling when people say: "We are building the church." How dare we say that! If we are building the church, no wonder the gates of Hades have overwhelmed us. There is no one who can build His church but Christ Himself. He is our High Priest building His church, and the way He is building is such that even John fell down as dead. Then he heard a voice. That is the testimony of our Lord Jesus concerning Himself.

## JESUS' TESTIMONY OF HIMSELF

### *He is the First, the Last, the Living One*

The Lord said, "I am the first and the last and the living One." That speaks of His deity. He is the first. Time-wise, even before the foundation of the world, He was there with the Father. He is the first, not only time-wise, but He is the first quality-wise because in Him all the fullness of the Godhead dwells.

The Lord Jesus is the last which means He is the end. He is what God is after. He concludes everything. He is the motive of everything. He gets the glory of everything. This is the testimony of Jesus. It is not just a proclamation or a word; it is a living Word. There is reality. Is He the first and the last in our lives?

God will not be satisfied unless His Son is the first in our lives. We have many relationships. Some seem to be closer to us than others, and we will even consider them as more valuable in our lives. But the Father's testimony to His Son is that His Son must be the first. This challenge of the Father challenges every believer. Have we ever been challenged by God about this matter? Is Christ the first in our life? We need to be honest before the Lord. Can we honestly say He is the first?

Not only that, He is the last. Is He the very motive, object, goal of our life? Do we have any other end or any other goal in our life? Think of Paul and how he despised everything for the excellency of the knowledge of Jesus Christ! He forgot what was behind and pressed on towards the goal which is Christ Himself.

Brothers and sisters, the testimony of Jesus is powerful. It is not just a word or slogan. It is a life. When our Lord Jesus says, "I am the first and I am the last," He means it. This is what He wants to be in each of our lives and in the church, and anything less than that will not satisfy Him. He is absolute.

He said, "I am the living One." Do we enjoy the life of our Lord Jesus? Do we find Him as the living One, as our very life? Are we living by His life? The apostle Paul said, "For me to live is Christ." Christ is the living One, not I. This is the testimony of Jesus. Do we have it?

### He Became Dead

Then He said, "I became dead." This speaks of His humanity. "The Word became flesh and tabernacled among men, full of grace and truth" (John 1:14). This is the Lord Jesus that we are familiar with. How He loves us! He denied Himself and died on the cross for us! He did it.

### I Am Living

"Behold I am living." This speaks of His resurrection and ascension. He is living. Christian faith is not an empty faith, it is not just a theological subject; it is living and real. Christ lives and therefore we live.

### I Am Living to the Ages of Ages

"Behold I am living to the ages of ages." That is eternal life.

### I Have the Keys to Death and Hades

"And I have the keys of death and Hades." In other words, He is the Conqueror. He has overcome death and Hades. He has cast out the one who holds the keys of death and Hades. The church is built on the victory of Christ.

The testimony of Jesus is that which we find in the book of Revelation. Do we have the testimony of Jesus?

## THE TESTIMONY OF JESUS IS NOT JUST WORDS WE SPEAK

You will remember that in Ephesus there were seven sons of the chief priest Sceva who were exorcists; they were doing the work of casting out demons. When they saw that Paul was powerful in casting out demons in the name of Jesus, they took that name and tried to cast out demons in the name of Christ whom Paul proclaimed. But the demons jumped upon two of the sons, stripped them naked, hurt them, and they had to flee.

Thus, we can see that the testimony of Jesus is not just a slogan we use. It is very, very real. The problem with many today is that it is a small thing. Do we have the testimony of Jesus? That is the reason why we have to go back again and again over this matter.

Dear brothers and sisters, we are living at a very exciting time. On the one hand, we know we are living at the end time, and everything is shaking. Not only is the earth shaking, the heaven is also shaking that the unshakeable may be brought into being. As we are living in this age, the testimony of Jesus is so important. John had the testimony of Jesus.

## DO NOT BE COMPLACENT ABOUT THIS MATTER—IT CONCERNS OUR FUTURE

So the question that is facing every one of us is this: can we be complacent? Our future, as it were, hangs upon this matter. Do we have the testimony of Jesus? Thank God, we are saved by His grace, but the testimony of Jesus is something that God is asking of every one of us.

One day, at the coming of our Lord Jesus, those who have the testimony of Jesus will enter into the kingdom of the heavens with Christ and will reign and rule with Him for a thousand years. Those who are saved but do not have the testimony of Jesus will not be able to enter into the joy of the Lord for a thousand years. Eventually, by the grace of God, they will also have the testimony of Jesus. In eternity we will all be gathered there as the servants of God.

This is what the Bible calls the gospel of the kingdom of the heavens. The end shall not come until the gospel of the kingdom of the heavens has been preached to all the nations. And dear brothers and sisters, this is what we are preaching this morning. So may the Lord have mercy on us.

Shall we pray:

*Dear Lord, we do praise and thank Thee that even at this last minute, Thou art still seeking us and pleading for us that we may not live a life that does not meet Thy eye, but we pray that by Thy grace we may have the testimony of Jesus just like the apostle John. We worship Thee; in Thy precious name. Amen.*

# CHAPTER 2: THE WAY OF THE TESTIMONY

*Revelation 1:9—I John, your brother and fellow-partaker in the tribulation and kingdom and patience, in Jesus, was in the island called Patmos, for the word of God, and for the testimony of Jesus.*

Let's have a word of prayer:

*Dear Lord, how we want to praise and thank Thee that people such as we are so privileged to sit with Thee and eat with Thee. We praise and thank Thee for all that Thou hast done for us. Thou hast captured our hearts. We are forever Thine. May Thy will be done in each and every one of our lives. We are here, Lord, bought with Thy price, and such a price Thou hast paid for us. Oh dear Lord, speak, and we will follow; in Thy precious name. Amen.*

We have just had the Lord's Table and my thought was this: How good it would be that as we are partaking in the Lord's Table, we enter into the marriage feast of the Lamb. That is our blessed hope.

We have been sharing together on God's testimony and way, and I hope we are convinced that there is nothing more important to us than God's testimony. We are bought with a price; therefore we do not live for ourselves. What is our aim? What is the meaning for our life? It is the testimony of Jesus.

The testimony of Jesus tells us who He is, and because of what He is, this should not just be a theory to us. It is life to us. If He is the beginning and the end and the living One, then He ought to be the first of our life and the last of our life. It ought to be that we no longer live for ourselves; it is Christ who lives in us. So whatever our Lord Jesus is, that is what we ought to be because it is He who lives in us. This is the testimony of Jesus.

## ENTERING INTO THE TESTIMONY

Now we would like to share together on this matter of the way: How do we enter into the testimony of Jesus? We find in the Scriptures those who have the testimony of Jesus. Are we among those people? If we have the desire to have the testimony of Jesus, then where is the way? How can we enter into it? In recent years, I deeply feel that it is not a matter of how much we know, it is not a matter of theological approach, but I deeply feel it is time that we should approach the whole matter from the practical standpoint. In other words, how can we experientially enter into the testimony of Jesus? Or to put it another way, in what practical way can the testimony of Jesus become our testimony?

In Revelation 1 the apostle John said, "I am your brother and fellow-partaker in the tribulation and kingdom and patience in Jesus" (see v. 9). John our brother was exiled to the island of Patmos for the Word of God and the testimony of Jesus. The Word of God refers to all that we find in the Old Testament. The testimony of Jesus is what we find in the New Testament. In other words, John was exiled for one reason and that was because he bore the testimony of Jesus. So I think we can learn from him in the most practical way of how we enter into the testimony of Jesus.

Among all the disciples of our Lord Jesus, the apostle John was one of the first who followed the Lord Jesus. In the Gospel of John we find that he was a disciple of John the Baptist. We know at that time among the Jewish people there were some who were really waiting for the Messiah to come. But it seems that even though the nation as a whole was waiting for the Messiah, unfortunately, the people were waiting for the Messiah for political reasons which were wrong. But there were a few among the Jewish people who were really waiting for the Messiah to come, and not only waiting, they were preparing the way for the coming of the Messiah. So even though John was a fisherman, he was not an ordinary fisherman because we find that in his business of fishing, his father had hired servants (see Mark 1:20) and he knew the high priest (see

John 18:15-16). So John, in a sense, was most unusual, but he had a heart for the Messiah.

## THE APOSTLE JOHN MEETS THE LORD JESUS

When John the Baptist came preaching that the kingdom of the heavens had drawn nigh and to repent, John responded and became a disciple of John the Baptist. One day while John was standing with his master, the Lord Jesus passed by. John the Baptist pointed to the Lord Jesus and said, "Behold, the Lamb of God." Immediately, John left John the Baptist and followed the Lord Jesus. He and Andrew were the first to follow the Lord. The Lord turned to them and said, "What do you want?" Brothers and sisters, they did not want more teaching; they wanted Him. They said, "Where do you live? We want to stay with You." During their time of staying with the Lord, they knew the Lord was the Messiah.

## SONS OF THUNDER

The apostle John was among the first who followed the Lord and became His disciple.

Among the twelve apostles, he was the last one to die; therefore, he had a long history with the Lord. And we also know from the Scriptures that among all of the disciples he was the closest to the Lord. We know that when the Lord called him and the other disciples, He gave some of them nicknames, and to the two sons of Zebedee, James and John, the Lord called them Boanerges, which means "Sons of Thunder." We are all familiar with thunder and when it strikes, it is terrible. Why did the Lord call James and John the Sons of Thunder? As we look at John, we find he was a very quiet and reserved person, and we would probably call him an introvert. It seems as if he was always very quiet but he was very watchful. He kept everything in his heart and pondered over them deeply. He was neither a shallow person nor a talkative person; he was deep. He was not an outgoing person but reserved and kept to himself. However, the Lord Jesus knew him and called him a Son of Thunder. In other words, we should not be deceived by his outward appearance, for things were being stored up within him until one day he strikes, and it was terrible. That is John.

## GOD LOVES VARIETY

The Lord has made every one of us differently. We know that our outward appearance is different. When we look at our face, which is only a small area, yet there are a number of features on our face. God can place all of these features in a small area, but each one is different. No one is the same. God really loves variety. But not only is our physical appearance different, even our soul has a shape, and every soul has a different shape. Some souls are extroverts, like Peter, who liked to talk. Others are introverts who turn inward and are quiet. Some are very quick; some are very slow. We are all different because our God loves variety. He does not want to make us uniform. That is why we should not imitate one another. Be what God has made you to be. That is beautiful, wonderful. But whether we are extroverts or introverts, the source is the same—Adam. There is no difference.

## THE WAY OF TESTIMONY IS DISCIPLESHIP

When you read about Peter in the Bible, you must really sympathize with him. The Lord Jesus dealt with him very severely because he was so outspoken. He was always trying to be the first to speak; therefore, He would be the first to be disciplined. As we learn the life of Peter, we find that he was deeply disciplined by the Lord, and oftentimes, we are sympathetic with him. "Peter, keep your mouth shut and you will be all right." On the other hand, John was very quiet. He moved around almost unnoticed but everything was in his heart. He was a Son of Thunder.

You remember the story in Luke 9 when our Lord Jesus was traveling and they encountered a person who was casting out demons in the name of the Lord. However, that person did not follow with the disciples as they followed Jesus. John came to the Lord and said, "Lord, we found a person casting out demons in Your name but he does not follow with us, so we forbade him" (see v. 54). In other words, they were very exclusive. You have to follow the Lord with us, otherwise you are out. And the Lord said, "He who is not against you is for you" (v. 50).

When the Lord passed through the villages of Samaria, one village would not receive Him because the Jews and Samaritans had nothing to do with each other especially when they were traveling to Jerusalem. Usually, when the Jews travelled from Galilee to Jerusalem, they would cross the river Jordan and travel on the other side until they came to Jerusalem. Nevertheless, our Lord Jesus passed through Samaria, but the village would not receive him. John and James were zealous for the Lord, and they came to Him and said, "Look! This village did not receive You. Will You allow us to cry to heaven to send down fire and consume them?" Outwardly, they were zealous for the Lord, but actually their heart was not right before the Lord. So the Lord said, "You do not know of what spirit you are. This is a wrong spirit." Our Lord came as a Lamb; that is His Spirit. But here we find that their spirit was opposite to the Spirit of the Lord.

The disciples' backgrounds were not very high class, so we find that they had been quarreling among themselves most of the time. They were thinking: Who is the greatest among us? Even at the Lord's Table we find them still quarrelling about who was the greatest. Then the sons of Zebedee called their mother to come, who, humanly speaking, was an aunt to our Lord Jesus. And we know the word of the aunt has some authority. At the last entry of our Lord Jesus into Jerusalem, they got their mother to come and speak to the Lord Jesus. She said, "I have a request. Promise You will answer me." I think she was a little shameful of asking for special treatment. In other words, she asked the Lord to sign a blank check. Thank God, our Lord never signs a blank check. But the Lord drew her out and said, "What do you really want?" She said, "When You sit on the throne (they thought the Lord was going to Jerusalem to be crowned), let my two sons sit, one on Your right and one on Your left." They got it all. No wonder the other ten were indignant. Our Lord said, "Are you able to drink the cup that I am drinking?" Without knowing what the cup really was they said, "We will." Our Lord said, "Yes, you have to drink the cup but to sit on My right and My left is not for Me to give; it is for My Father to give." And the other ten disciples were indignant because they were outmaneuvered.

So brothers and sisters, whether we are an introvert or extrovert, before God it is the same because it is the Adamic life that is in us. Therefore, do not think that because John was such a lovely fellow, he was not disciplined as much by the Lord. No, the Lord dealt with them all very seriously.

## DISCIPLESHIP MEANS BEING UNDER DISCIPLINE

Why do I mention this? It is because the way to have the testimony of Jesus is the way of discipleship, and discipleship means being under discipline. I know this word discipline is something we do not like, especially in our times. We want everything to be free. The parents are not allowed to discipline their children, and teachers are not allowed to discipline the students. Let everyone grow freely. But when we read the Word of God, we find that discipline is God's love. If you love your children, then you will discipline your children. Without discipline, we cannot be saved from Adam, and we are not able to follow the Lord. This is the only way.

## THE WAY OF TESTIMONY IS THE CROSS

What is the way to have the testimony of Jesus? It is not by sitting in a sedan chair and being taken to heaven. That is not the way. The way is to deny self, take up your cross, and follow the Lord. I know this is not a popular way; people do not like it. Naturally speaking, no one loves discipline. We want to be on our own, stand on our own feet, stand for our own rights; that is the way we are. Nevertheless, the only way to have the testimony of Jesus is through the cross. Without the cross, there is no crown. Even though it is unpopular, the Word of God makes it very clear that this is the way. Are we traveling this way?

## THE GREAT COMMISSION

I believe we are all familiar with the great commission which is found in Matthew 28. Before our Lord ascended to heaven, He gave His church a great commission. Thank God, because of this great commission, people went to distant countries to preach the gospel of grace, to seek and to save the lost. But I am afraid we have misunderstood the great commission that the

Lord has given to the church. It is true, evangelism is basic because if people are not evangelized, if they have not believed in the Lord Jesus, how can they be disciplined? How can they be disciples? Today, we make believers and disciples two different people. In other words, you can be a believer and not a disciple of the Lord Jesus. When you read the Bible, we find that believers and disciples are one and the same thing. If you believe in the Lord Jesus, if you have received Him as your Savior, if you have enjoyed all the salvation that He has given to you, does it mean that it makes you more self-centered, more for yourself? On the contrary, because we have received such mercy and grace from our Lord Jesus, our only response can be this: "Brethren, by the mercies of God, I beseech you to present your bodies a living sacrifice, holy, acceptable to God, which is your worship and service" (see Romans 12:1).

Brothers and sisters, we who have been saved have no right to live for ourselves. Whatever profession we may have, we are to live for Christ. We are His disciples. So the great commission is to go to the nations and disciple them. It is not just to evangelize them, which is included, but that is not the end. God wants His church to disciple all nations.

What does discipling mean? I am afraid there is much misunderstanding about discipling. I remember in the sixties there was quite a movement in America called the Charismatic movement and many people got saved. In Fort Lauderdale there were seven dear brothers who loved the Lord and were very gifted. The Lord began to reveal to these seven brothers one thing after another. They were so capable that whatever the Lord showed them, they tried to make it work. At one time the Lord showed them discipleship, and they put it into practice at once. They began to arrange people in pairs, putting one over another. One would be the lord and the other a disciple. It spread over the nations, crossing denominations. When one was put under a master, there were different stages they had to go through. And these seven brothers were at the top as apostles. They controlled everything in the lives of these people; not only their spiritual life but even their daily family life. This caused such a problem in the Charismatic movement that it nearly split it because they were not discipling people to Christ but to man.

I often say our soul is so precious to our God that He will not commit it to anyone else. He alone is responsible for our souls. Yes, we do need help. We need people to help us to Christ—not to themselves. But it is Christ and only Christ.

## DISCIPLED TO CHRIST—NOT TO MAN

In the early days, there was no school system such as we have today in which students pay to go to school and teachers or professors are employed to teach them. If you wanted to learn a trade you would find a master—maybe a carpenter or someone else who was skillful—and you signed a contract. When you were apprenticed to your master, you would leave your home and stay with your master as if you are one of the members of the family. Usually, during the first year, he would not even allow you to touch the instruments of his trade. During the first year you stayed with this family, you served them. You swept the floor, helped with the children, brought food to your master. You were as a slave or a servant in the family. But you might say, "I came to learn the trade, so what has all of this to do with me?" Basically, this is how it must be because you are not only learning a trade; you are learning a life. After you have finished your training, not only do you have the skill of your master, but you walk like your master, you speak like your master, and you act like your master. His character begins to characterize you. This is discipleship.

## DISCIPLESHIP BEGINS WITH BAPTISM

Brothers and sisters, we are not going to the school of Christ; we are going to the gymnasium of Christ. It is not just a mental exercise; it is a spiritual exercise. Why is it that our Lord Jesus said in the great commission: "Go to the nations and disciple them, baptizing them in the name of the Father, the Son, and the Holy Spirit?" Why does discipleship begin with baptism? People often say, "I believe in the Lord Jesus, am I not saved?" Thank God, we are. Why should we be baptized? In baptism, we give ourselves up. When we enter the water, it symbolizes that we are dead with Christ. When we are under the water, we are buried with Christ. When we come out of the water, we are risen with Christ. In other words, when we are baptized, we give ourselves totally up. As we come out of the water, it is no longer I; it is Christ who lives in us. We have surrendered our life and our rights to the Lord. Baptism is a declaration of faith. We declare that we are so constrained by the love of Christ that we give ourselves totally over to Him. That is the beginning of discipleship, and this is what consecration really means.

## A LIVING SACRIFICE

Why does the Bible tell us that it is by the manifold mercies of God as described in Romans chapters 1-11? Who can measure the mercies of God that have been poured out upon us? Hence, what is our response? We are to present our bodies voluntarily out of love as a living sacrifice. Why does it say "our bodies?" It is because it is through our bodies that we live our life. In other words, consecration is for every believer. No one is to believe and not consecrate their bodies because the very fact of being saved shows that we are no longer ours; we are His.

That is the beginning and not the end. Thank God, when we believe in the Lord Jesus, that is not the end; that is the beginning. From that day onward, our Lord, by His indwelt Holy Spirit, will begin to work in us to put the old Adamic life to death and put Christ Jesus in us to grow until we are transformed and conformed to His image.

Brothers and sisters, this is the way to have the testimony of Jesus. The apostle John traveled this way. This is the way open to every one of us. Are we on the way? Our Lord Jesus set before us Himself as an example—how He lived on this earth, denying Himself all the time, submitting Himself totally to the will of His Father even unto death and that is the death of the cross. The Lord said, "Follow Me. Take My yoke upon you and learn of Me. For I am meek and lowly in heart, and you shall find rest in your souls" (see Matthew 11:28-30).

Brothers and sisters, naturally we are all wild animals. We have our own thoughts, our own ideas, our own determinations, our own will, and our own way. We need to learn of Christ. How do we learn of Him? Yoke with Him. Then we shall find rest in our souls. This is discipleship.

Dear brothers and sisters, hopefully every one of us will answer the call of discipleship, giving ourselves to the Lord, and allowing Him to work Christ into us until we are conformed to His image. May the Lord have mercy upon us!

Shall we pray:

*Dear Lord, Thou hast done all for us. What can we do for You? There is nothing we can do but give ourselves over to You and allow You to work out Your marvelous salvation and Your purpose until we are transformed and conformed to Your image to the praise of Your glory. We ask in Thy name. Amen.*

# CHAPTER 3:
# QUESTIONS & ANSWERS

I hope you are not disappointed with this session. All man can do is help us to solve some mental block. Other than that man can do nothing. So if you have any real spiritual problems, go to the Lord Himself. Otherwise, your problem will never be solved.

Q. How will the Lord discipline us? Can you give an illustration from the Word? What are the ways the Lord uses to discipline us to be His disciple? I think these two questions are closely related.

A. As we read the Word of God we will find that there are plenty of illustrations how the Lord Jesus dealt with His disciples. How did He discipline His disciples? In other words, unless our Lord Jesus disciplines us, He is not treating us as His children. So you find in Hebrews 12 it says, "It is the love of the Father that disciplines his son. If you are without discipline, then you are a bastard and not a son" (see vv. 6-8). So I think our mentality has to be changed. We need to see discipline as love and not hatred. It is because of the love of God that He condescends Himself to discipline us in order to bring us out of ourselves and into Christ.

## GOD'S DISCIPLINE IS ACCORDING TO OUR SPIRITUAL CONDITION

God's way of disciplining us is according to our spiritual condition. Therefore, in the beginning of our Christian life, usually He will discipline us in something that is more outward. For instance, probably we have the habit of sleeping late, and when we get up we have no time for our daily devotion. So with only a few minutes we try to pray or even read the Word before we go out to school or work.

I remember Miss Groves, who was a companion of Miss Barber, said, "The problem between God and man is over the bed—whether in the morning you can get up earlier to have time with the Lord. That is a problem." So I believe that when our Lord Jesus is disciplining us, in the beginning it will come to you as a matter over your bed. Maybe the Lord by His Spirit is moving in you and challenging you. Do you so love your body? Are you able to put your body under to obey you instead of letting your body be your master? Now it seems to be a very small thing but probably your spiritual life depends upon it. So usually, when the Lord is disciplining us He begins with something outward and small, and then gradually He will begin to challenge us with something deeper. In a sense, when we are talking about the discipline of the Lord, usually the Holy Spirit will so arrange our environment and use it to deal with different things in our lives.

## OUR EMOTIONS NEED TO BE DISCIPLINED

In Matthew 10 we find that when our Lord Jesus first sent His disciples out, He told them He was sending them out as sheep among the wolves. Then in Matthew 10:37 He said, "If you love your father, mother, brother or sister, or yourself more than Me, you cannot be My disciple." In other words, the Lord is dealing with the emotional life. We all have our emotions, and to love our father, mother, brother, sister, wife, husband, children is good; it is natural. We are even commanded to respect and love our parents, and this is the one commandment with promise. But unfortunately, after man fell his self-life was so fallen that it had to be delivered. In order to deliver us from our self-life, that is, from our soul-life, He has to deal with the emotion of our soul-life because it is the most evident expression of our soul. There is nothing more important than love or hate. If we love the right thing and hate the wrong thing, then we are on the right path. Otherwise, if we hate what we should love and we love what we should hate, then something is drastically wrong. So usually when God is dealing with us, He will deal first of all with our emotional life.

There is something commendable in loving our parents; nevertheless, the Lord's demand is this: "If you love your father or mother more than Me you cannot be My disciple." The reason for this is that the emotion of our soul-life has to be changed. It does not mean that if you love the Lord more than your parents then you do not love your parents. On the contrary, if you love the Lord more than your father or mother you will love your parents more in the right way. And usually in our early days God will deal with us in this area.

## WHY IS BAPTISM NECESSARY?

I remember when I was a young Christian, the Lord dealt with me on this matter of baptism. I was baptized when I was a baby, but after I was saved I was told that I needed to be baptized according to the Word of God by immersion. I always opposed that because I told people that when my father baptized me in the name of the Father, Son and Holy Spirit I was baptized. Therefore, I should not use the name of God in an idle way. But gradually, as I was reading the Bible, more and more I was convinced that one has to believe first and then be baptized. Inwardly, I was touched by the Word of God, but outwardly, I was still resisting it because I loved my father, who was a Methodist pastor. He loved the Lord and I loved him. If I were to be baptized by immersion, what would happen to my father? I could not do that. But again and again the Holy Spirit worked in my life until one day a brother began to talk to me about baptism. Inwardly, I knew it was true, but outwardly, I was still very strong and persistent in resisting it. So that brother gave me up and said I was hopeless and left me alone.

One day, I remember very vividly sitting by myself and praying. I said, "Lord, I know I should be baptized by immersion but this is not the time. I promise You after I graduate from college, after I am independent, then I will be baptized. Then I heard a voice speaking to me: "He who loves his father or mother cannot be My disciple." This was the first time I heard a voice as if somebody was talking to me. There was nobody around, and when that Word came to me with such power, I told the Lord: "I will be baptized."

I came down from my friend's room, went next door where brother Watchman Nee was living, and I knocked at the door. He came out and said to me: "What do you want?" I said, "I want to be baptized." He said, "Does your father know?" He knew my father. I said, "I have not told my father yet, but I feel the Lord has called me to do so." And by the grace of God I was baptized the next day.

Why have I mentioned this? This was the beginning of my spiritual life. Before that day I was zealous for the Lord, and I was serving the Lord according to my will. But that day God began to open my eyes, and it was the beginning of my spiritual journey.

Our emotional life needs to be delivered. Who controls our emotional life? It is I, myself. However, the discipline of the Lord is to allow Christ to be in charge of my soul. Instead of my soul expressing myself it will be expressing Christ, for He will sit on the throne of my soul. That is discipline; that is purification; that is transformation; that is to be conformed to the image of Christ.

## OUR MIND NEEDS TO BE DISCIPLINED

In Matthew 16, after Peter confessed the Lord Jesus as Christ, the Son of the living God, the Lord began to tell His disciples that He would go to Jerusalem and be crucified. Then Peter took hold of the Lord and said, "Lord, it should never happen to You. Be mindful of Yourself." Peter did it in good will, with good intention, and yet he was out of the will of God. Then the Lord turned around and said, "Satan, get thee behind Me because you are not mindful of God but of man." In other words, here is an illustration of how our mind needs to be disciplined. Instead of self using the mind it will be Christ expressing Himself through our mind. That is the result of discipline.

## OUR WILL NEEDS TO BE DISCIPLINED

When our Lord Jesus was in the garden of Gethsemane, He was in tremendous conflict (see Matthew 26). He who knew no sin was to be made sin for us. Humanly speaking, He could not bear it. He asked the Father: "If it is possible let this cup be removed from Me but not My will; Thy will be done." Then He prayed, "If it is Thy will let it be done." In other words, our will needs to be disciplined. Unless our will is disciplined we are the master of our life, but if our will Is disciplined and we let God's will be our will, then there is the salvation of the soul.

## GOD DISCIPLINES OUT OF LOVE

There are so many cases we can find in the Scriptures of how the Lord will discipline us, but it is always out of love. When such discipline comes to us in whatever area it might be, so far as we ourselves are concerned it is impossible. Who does not love himself? Who does not want to be on his own? Who does not want to have his will? It is only when we are constrained by the love of Christ that we can submit to the discipline. It is the only way. We ourselves cannot fight against ourselves. No man can lift himself up; it is impossible. But thank God when the discipline of the Lord is the love of Christ, then we can receive it from His hand. Therefore, when we are constrained by the love of Christ, nothing is impossible.

So brothers and sisters, these are the ways that the Lord will deal with us. Do not think it is only by some spectacular way, but in our daily life, in small things as well as big things, the Lord is purifying us. He is saving our soul. He is delivering us from ourselves into Christ. You know, our greatest enemy is not Satan; it is ourselves. Martin Luther said, "I am not afraid of the Pope, the cardinals, and all these others, but I am afraid of the pope within me.

## IF YOU LOVE YOUR SOUL YOU WILL LOSE IT

Brothers and sisters, in our spiritual progress, sooner of later, we will be faced with this matter of discipline. If we reject it we are still saved, but barely saved. However, if we are willing to give ourselves up and allow the Lord to have His way with us, then our soul will be delivered. So our Lord Jesus said, "If you love your soul you will lose it. If you lose it for my sake, you will gain it to eternity." So I think probably this will remove any hindrance to our spiritual progress.

## INITIAL SALVATION IS OF THE SPIRIT

When we believe in the Lord Jesus, we are saved. But which part of us was saved? It was not our body because after we believed in the Lord Jesus we discovered that we were still in this mortal body. Of course, there was a little change, and I often say it is from a long face to a round face; but that is superficial. Even though we are saved we are still in this mortal body, and we are affected by the environment around us. We can still get sick. When we were saved in the beginning, was our soul saved at the same time? No, you are still you, and I am still me. In the beginning it seems as if we had been delivered because in our first love we were really riding on a cloud. And at that time if the Lord demanded anything from us, we would give it to Him. That is our first love. But gradually we fall down and begin to discover we are even stronger than God.

When we were first saved, what was it that was saved? It was our spirit because it was dead in sins and transgressions. Our spirit had lost its communication with God, but when we are saved, not only were our sins forgiven which is negative, but positively, the Lord has given us a new spirit. Our human spirit that was dead in sins and transgressions has been renewed; it has awakened. In Ezekiel we find that we have a new spirit in which the Holy Spirit comes and dwells.

## CHRIST DWELLS IN OUR SPIRIT

We say that Christ dwells in us. But where does He dwell? Is it in our body or in our soul? No, He dwells in our spirit. Therefore, we find that what we usually call salvation refers to our spirit. Something marvelous has happened in our spirit. Our communication with God has been renewed. Christ becomes the life of our spirit and the Holy Spirit is there to see to it that this life of Christ will grow into maturity. That is the work of the indwelling Holy Spirit. So that is what we usually call salvation or initial salvation. That is not the end; it is the beginning. And after we are saved, why is it that the Lord does not just rapture us to heaven? I often feel how glorious, how good it would be if the moment I was saved I was raptured; it would save me from all the trouble that I have been going through. But the love of God is otherwise. He loves us so much He leaves us in this wretched world to go through things to save our soul.

## SALVATION OF THE SOUL

Brothers and sisters, after we believe in the Lord Jesus, why is it that the Lord still leaves us on earth? If He loves us should He not take us immediately to Himself? No, because He loves us He leaves us here. I thank God for leaving me so long because He loves me. He wants to complete His work. Thank God that every day we are living He is still giving us opportunity. Salvation of the soul is for today. Daily He is working to save our soul from ourselves and to replace self with Christ; this is the work that is going on today. Every day is precious, every day is opportunity, every day is training, every day the Holy Spirit is arranging our circumstances, every day the Spirit of God dwells in us and is speaking to us. He is putting us to the cross and forming Christ in us. Christian life is really exciting. How we moan when we are disciplined but actually we should praise Him when we are disciplined. If we are disciplined it shows He is still loving us. If He lets us go it shows we are hopeless. So the salvation of the soul is for today. God is working in us. Whom He has called He has justified, whom He has justified, He will glorify. And glorify simply means to be like Christ, build His character into our lives that we may live by the life of Christ in us and not by ourselves.

Q. Can such salvation of the soul be completed before our mortal body dies?

A. It can and it should. When Paul wrote the letter to the Philippians, he said, "I do not say I have arrived. I am forgetting what is behind and stretching out myself towards the goal that is before me." But when he wrote II Timothy before his martyrdom, he could say, "I have finished the course, I have fought the good fight, I have kept the faith. Therefore, a crown of righteousness is waiting for me—not only for me but for all who love the Lord" (see II Timothy 4:7-8). So from II Timothy we can safely say and I hope it will be real to each and every one of us that we may also declare: "I have finished the race." Thank God for that.

Q. Under what condition do we fully cooperate with the Holy Spirit to carry the cross daily?

A. There is only one condition required of us—absolute surrender. That is why in Romans we find after eleven chapters that tell us of the mercies of God, our response is to present our bodies a living sacrifice. This is holy and acceptable to God and it is our reasonable service and spiritual worship. So the only one condition that is required on our part is absolute surrender, and all the other works are being done by God Himself. That is grace.

So may the Lord help us.

# Other Books Printed By
# Christian Testimony Ministry

| SPEAKER | TITLE |
|---|---|
| DANA CONGDON | MARRIAGE, SINGLENESS, AND THE WILL OF GOD |
| | RECOVERY & RESTORATION |
| | THE HOLY SPIRIT |
| | HEBREWS |
| | |
| A.J. FLACK | TENT OF HIS SPLENDOUR |
| | |
| STEPHEN KAUNG | ACTS |
| | BE YE THEREFORE PERFECT |
| | CALLED OUT UNTO CHRIST |
| | CALLED TO THE FELLOWSHIP OF GOD'S SON |
| | DIVINE LIFE AND ORDER |
| | FOR ME TO LIVE IS CHRIST |
| | GLORIOUS LIBERTY OF THE CHILDREN OF GOD |
| | GOD'S PURPOSE FOR THE FAMILY |
| | I WILL BUILD MY CHURCH |
| | MEDITATIONS ON THE KINGDOM |
| | RECOVERY |
| | SPIRITUAL EXERCISE |
| | SPIRITUAL LIFE (II CORINTHIANS SERIES) |
| | TEACH US TO PRAY |
| | THE CROSS |
| | THE FULNESS OF CHRIST—IN THE BOOK OF REVELATION |
| | THE HEADSHIP OF CHRIST |
| | THE KINGDOM AND THE CHURCH |
| | THE KINGDOM OF GOD |
| | THE LAST CALL TO THE CHURCHES, THE CALL TO OVERCOME |
| | THE LIFE OF OUR LORD JESUS |
| | THE LIFE OF THE CHURCH, THE BODY OF CHRIST |
| | THE LORD'S TABLE |
| | TWO GUIDEPOSTS FOR INHERITING THE KINGDOM |
| | VISION OF CHRIST (REVELATION) |
| | WHO ARE WE? |

WHY DO WE SO GATHER?
WORSHIP

LANCE LAMBERT          CALLED UNTO HIS ETERNAL GLORY
GOD'S ETERNAL PURPOSE
IN THE DAY OF THY POWER
JACOB I HAVE LOVED
LIVING FAITH
LESSONS FROM THE LIFE OF MOSES
LOVE DIVINE
MY HOUSE SHALL BE A HOUSE OF PRAYER
PREPARATION FOR THE COMING OF THE LORD
REIGNING WITH CHRIST
SPIRITUAL CHARACTER
THE GOSPEL OF THE KINGDOM
THE IMPORTANCE OF COVERING
THE LAST DAYS AND GOD'S PRIORITIES
THE PRIZE
THE SUPREMACY OF JESUS CHRIST
THINE IS THE POWER!
THOU ART MINE

T. AUSTIN-SPARKS        THE LORD'S TESTIMONY AND THE WORLD NEED


HARVEY CEDARS CONFERENCE

STEPHEN KAUNG          HEAVENLY VISION
SPIRITUAL RESPONSIBILITY

CONGDON, HILE, KAUNG    SPIRITUAL MINISTRY
SPIRITUAL AUTHORITY
SPIRITUAL HOUSE
SPIRITUAL SUBMISSION

STEPHEN KAUNG          SPIRITUAL KNOWLEDGE
SPIRITUAL POWER
SPIRITUAL REALITY
SPIRITUAL VALUE
SPIRITUAL BLESSING
SPIRITUAL DISCERNMENT